History Makers

Mary Seacole

... and the Crimean War

Sarah Ridley

This edition 2013

First published in 2009 by
Franklin Watts
338 Euston Road
London NW1 3BH

Franklin Watts Australia
Level 17/207 Kent Street
Sydney NSW 2000
Copyright © Franklin Watts 2009

ISBN: 978 1 4451 1795 9
Dewey classification: 610.73'092

Series editor: Jeremy Smith
Art director: Jonathan Hair
Design: Simon Morse
Cover design: Jonathan Hair
Picture research: Sarah Ridley

Picture credits: Bridgeman Art Library:
22. Bridgeman Art Library/Getty
Images: front cover background.
Collection Municipal Archives of
Rotterdam: 13. Mary Evans PL: 4.
Roger Fenton/Hulton Archive/Getty
Images: 11. Getty Images: 21.
Hulton Archive/Getty Images: 12, 19.
Museum of London: 7. National
Army Museum London/Bridgeman
Art Library: 10. Print Collector/
HIP/Topfoto: 6.Private Collection/
Bridgeman Art Library: 1, 9, 15.
Amoret Tanner Collection/Foto Libra:
front cover r, 2, 23.Time & Life
Pictures/Getty Images: 17. Wellcome
Library London, Wellcome Images: 5,
14, 18.

A CIP catalogue record for this book
is available from the British Library

Franklin Watts is a division of
Hachette Children's Books, an
Hachette UK company.
www.hachette.co.uk

Printed in China

Contents

Childhood

Mary Seacole was born in 1805 in Kingston, Jamaica. Her mother was Jamaican and her father was a Scottish soldier.

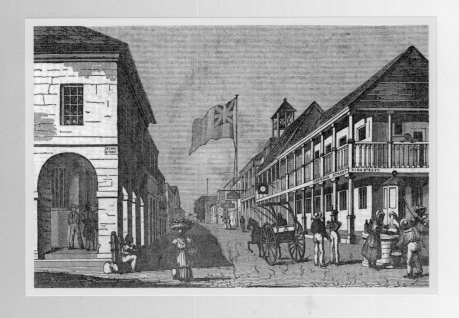

A drawing of Kingston in 1835. It is the capital of Jamaica.

February
1805 ▶

Mary Jane Grant, later to marry Edwin Seacole, is born.

A page from a book about healing plants. Mary learnt about these from her mother.

Her mother ran a small hotel and healed people with medicines she made from local plants. Mary often helped her mother.

1805 ▶

King George III reigns in Great Britain.
He ruled from 1760 to 1820.

The Empire

Jamaica was part of the British Empire. All over the Empire, the British army had camps. Mary and her mother nursed ill soldiers from the camp close to Kingston.

The British soldiers lived at Up-Park Camp, set in parkland close to Kingston.

1820 ▶

George IV becomes King of Great Britain.

1820 ▶

Florence Nightingale is born.

▲ A London street in 1822. Mary would have stood out as few black people lived there at this time.

Mary longed to see England, the country where the soldiers were born. Luckily, some relatives took Mary with them to visit London.

1820s ▶

Mary visits London twice.

1830 ▶

William IV becomes King of Great Britain.

Marriage

Back in Jamaica, Mary married Edwin Seacole. They ran a hotel together but Edwin was often ill. He died eight years later.

After a while, Mary decided to visit her brother in Panama. There, a terrible illness called cholera struck. Mary threw herself into nursing the sick.

1836 ▶
Mary marries Edwin Seacole, the godson of Admiral Nelson.

1837 ▶
Queen Victoria begins her reign.

1851-52 ▶
Mary visits Panama.

This drawing of Mary was done when she was in her forties.

1853 ▶

Mary nurses soldiers in Jamaica.

July
1853 ▶

The Crimean War begins.

1854 ▶

Mary returns to Panama.

9

The Crimean War

In 1854 Britain and France joined Turkey in a war against Russia in the Crimea. The Crimea is now part of Ukraine.

▲ The Battle of Balaclava in the Crimea.

March
1854 ▶
Britain joins the Crimean War.

October
1854 ▶
The Battle of Balaclava.

▲ A British army camp in the Crimea.

Soon the newspapers were full of stories about battles and wounded soldiers. Many soldiers also fell ill in the army camps.

1854 ▶

Florence Nightingale takes some nurses to the Crimea.

November
1854 ▶

The Battle of the Inkerman – many soldiers are wounded.

To the Crimea

Mary decided she must go and nurse the soldiers in the Crimea. She sailed to London and hoped to be sent out to join Florence Nightingale.

▶ This is a picture of Florence Nightingale. She took a group of nurses out to the Crimea.

1854 ▶

Mary arrives in London.

Sadly, Mary's help was rejected and she realised that the colour of her skin was stopping people from trusting her. In the end, she used her own money to set off for the Crimean War.

Mary travelled aboard this steamship called the *Hollander*.

1855 ▶

Mary travels to the Crimea.

The British Hotel

When she arrived, Mary went to visit Florence Nightingale at the army hospital. Then she joined her business partner, Thomas Day, and they set up the British Hotel.

Mary spent one night at the huge army hospital at Scutari.

January
1855 ▶

Mary arrives in the Crimea and visits Florence.

This drawing shows the inside of the British Hotel. Mary is the woman wearing a hat.

At the British Hotel, Mary sold food, useful goods and hot meals, and rented rooms to people. She nursed the soldiers' wounds and treated their illnesses.

March
1855

The British Hotel opens.

Florence

Meanwhile Florence Nightingale and her nurses were improving the army hospital. Now it was cleaner, more organised and the soldiers were better treated.

1855 ▶

Fewer soldiers are dying at the army hospital in Scutari.

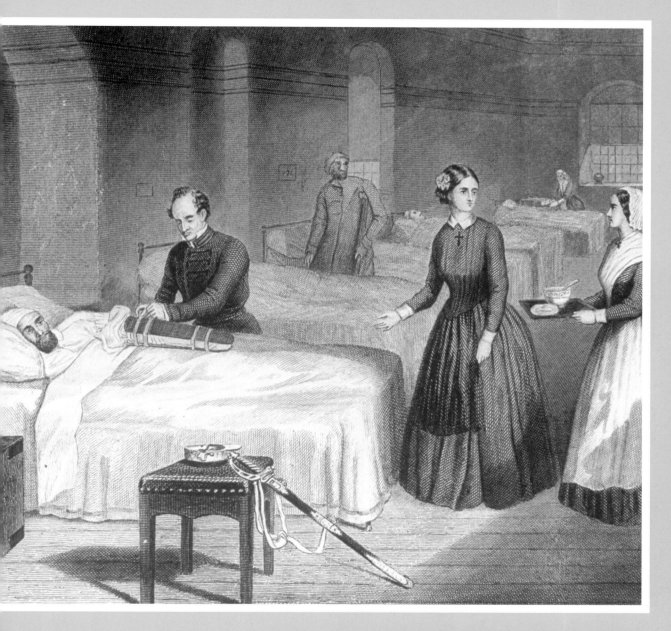

Florence visited the wards at night. The soldiers called her 'the lady with the lamp'.

'Mother Seacole'

Mary treated the sick wherever she could. Sometimes she packed up food and medicines and went to the battlefields to care for wounded soldiers.

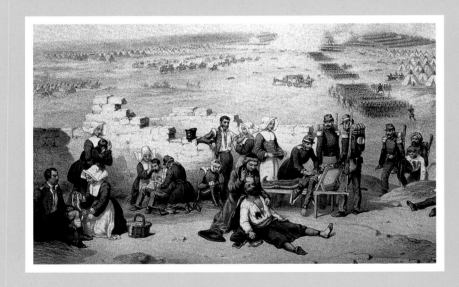

Like these nuns, Mary nursed wounded soldiers on the battlefield.

1855 ▶

Mary cares for British, French and Russian soldiers.

Other days she visited soldiers in their tents, or in nearby hospitals. Many soldiers called her 'Mother Seacole', to show their love for her.

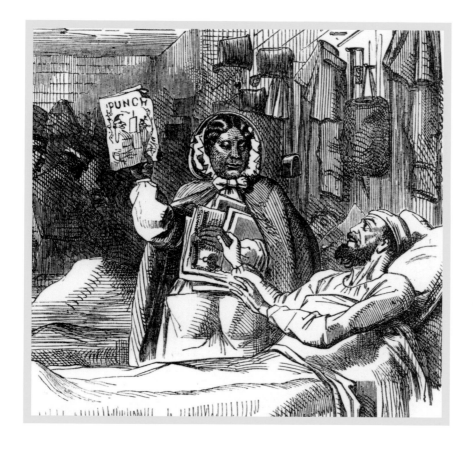

Mary visited men at a small hospital nearby. She tried to cheer them up as well as make them better.

December
1855 ▶

Mary serves Christmas lunch to soldiers at the British Hotel.

Return to England

The Crimean War ended in 1856, with Britain on the winning side. When Mary returned to England, she was famous but poor. Some of her old friends in the army raised money to help her.

This portrait shows Mary wearing the medals she was given for her work in the Crimea.

March 1856	October 1856
The Crimean War ends. Russia loses.	Mary returns to England.

November
1856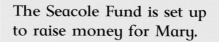

The Seacole Fund is set up
to raise money for Mary.

Mary's book

Mary's next project was to write a book about her life called *Wonderful Adventures of Mrs Seacole in Many Lands*. The book was a great success.

▲ Mary's book was published in 1857.

1857 ►
Wonderful Adventures of Mrs Seacole in Many Lands is published.

1860 ►
Mary returns to Jamaica.

1867 ►
Another fund raises money for Mary.

There is just one photo of Mary, this one, taken when she was an old lady.

After Mary died in 1881, people almost forgot about her. Slowly this has changed and, in 2004, she was named 'greatest black Briton'.

1870 ▶
Mary moves back to England.

1881 ▶
Mary dies.

2004 ▶
Mary is named 'greatest black Briton'.

Glossary

Admiral Nelson A famous British naval captain.

British Empire The countries ruled from Britain.

Capital The capital city is the main city of a country and its centre of government.

Crimean War (1853-1856) The war between Britain, France and Turkey on one side, Russia on the other.

Florence Nightingale Famous for her work in the Crimea, hospital reforms and for setting up a school of nursing.

Jamaica A Caribbean island, once part of the British Empire.

Panama A small country in Central America.

Wards The name for a room full of beds and patients in a hospital.

Index